JOHN LESLEY

CONTINENTS OF THE WORLD

South America

REDBACK publishing

Economy of South America p.24

The Amazon p.14

Redback Publishing
Suite 6, 13a Narabang Way,
Belrose NSW 2085
Australia

www.redbackpublishing.com
orders@redbackpublishing.com

ISBN 978-1-761401-00-8

Author: John Lesley
Editor: Caroline Thomas
Designer: Redback Publishing

Originated by Redback Publishing

Acknowledgements:
Abbreviations: l–left, r–right, b–bottom, t–top, c–centre, m–middle
We would like to thank the following for permission to reproduce photographs (images © Shutterstock unless otherwise stated):
p11tr Brazil, Ronaldo Almeida, p11mr Colombia, juangonzalez, p11bl Falkland Islands, Passion Travel Fruit, p11mr Argentina, Milton Ekman, p12b Cotopaxi, Ecuador, Fotos593, p13b Nevado del Ruíz, Colombia, The NASA Expedition 23 crew, Public domain, via Wikimedia Commons, p15bc moonseed plant, Nadiatalent, CC BY-SA 4.0 (https://creativecommons.org/licenses/by-sa/4.0), via Wikimedia Commons, p16br Statue of Pachacuti, videobuzzing, p17tr Peruvians, meunierd, p18t Rio Carnival, Celso Pupo, p18bl Festival of the Virgin of Candelaria, Don Mammoser, p27tr Uros Island, Lake Titicaca, Pakhnyushchy, p30tl Bogota, Colombia, Mark Pitt Images, p30ml Lima, Peru, Simon Mayer, p30bl Santiago, Chile, DFLC Prints, p20mr Sao Paulo, Brazil, Diego Grandi, p30br Buenos Aires, Argentina, Guaxinim, p32tl Rio Carnival, Celso Pupo

NATIONAL LIBRARY OF AUSTRALIA
A catalogue record for this book is available from the National Library of Australia

Contents

Agriculture p.25

Nature's Bounty p.22

People of South America p.16

Earth's 7 Continents

What is a continent?

Continents are very large landmasses that are separated from each other on Earth. Some continents are separated by oceans, but others have land borders with neighbouring continents.

How many continents are there on Earth?

There are seven continents

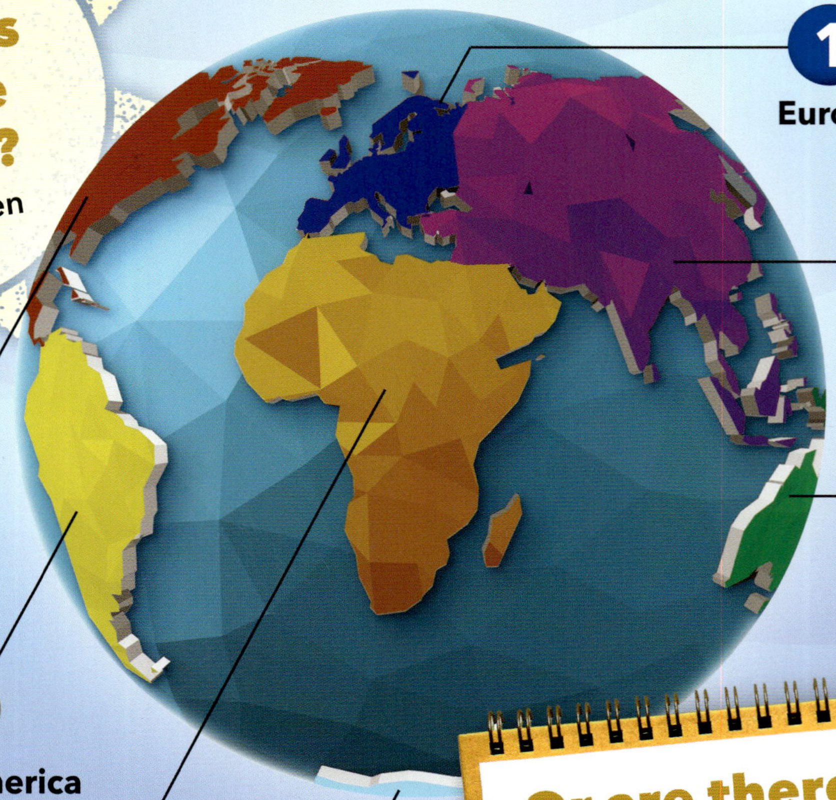

Or are there 5?

Some people group Europe and Asia into one continent called Eurasia, and they combine North and South America into the Americas. According to this method of counting, there are five continents instead of seven.

Origin of South America

How did the continents form?

The surface of our planet is constantly moving in a very slow process known as plate tectonics. The plates are gigantic slabs of rock that form the surface of our Earth. These plates rest on magma that is hotter and more liquid as it gets deeper towards the Earth's centre. As the heat rises out towards the surface of the Earth, it causes the plates to move around.

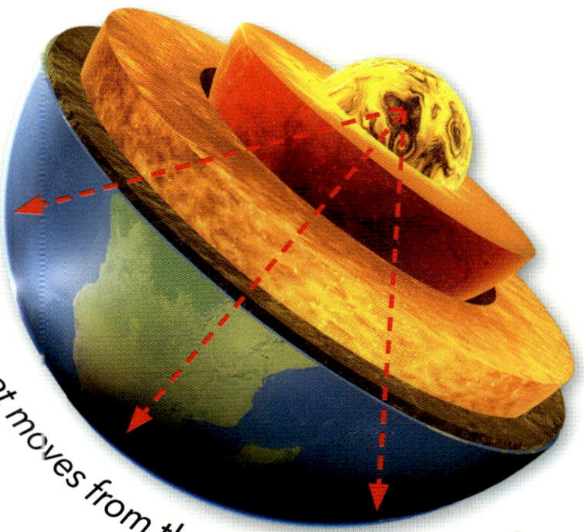
Heat moves from the centre to the surface

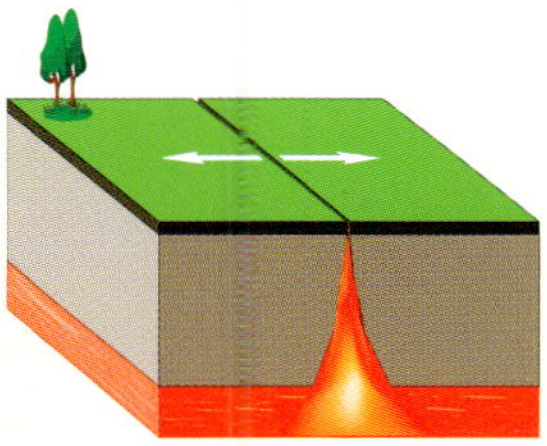
Plates pull apart

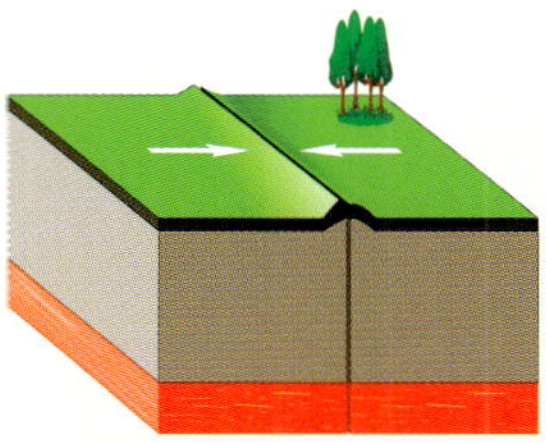
Plates push together

When these plates move, their edges can either pull apart or push together. Where the plates pull apart, oceans can flow between the landmasses, and where they push together, mountain ranges can form. This process explains how continents form over very long periods of time.

Pangaea

The continents were not always in the same location as they are now. Millions of years ago, they were parts of other huge masses of land. The one called Pangaea eventually broke apart, producing a number of landmasses, one of which is South America.

When it was part of Pangaea, the whole east coast of South America was joined to what is now Africa.

South America's Continental Shelves

Where a continent is bounded by an ocean, the land at the ocean's edge often continues under the water as a continental shelf. This shelf may end abruptly at a point where the underwater rocks drop down to a deep ocean abyss.

During the last Ice Age, which ended about 10,000 years ago, the world's sea levels were lower than they are now. At that time, some of South Americas's continental shelves were dry land, making the continent much bigger than it is today.

The Perito Moreno Glacier in Santa Cruz Province, Argentina

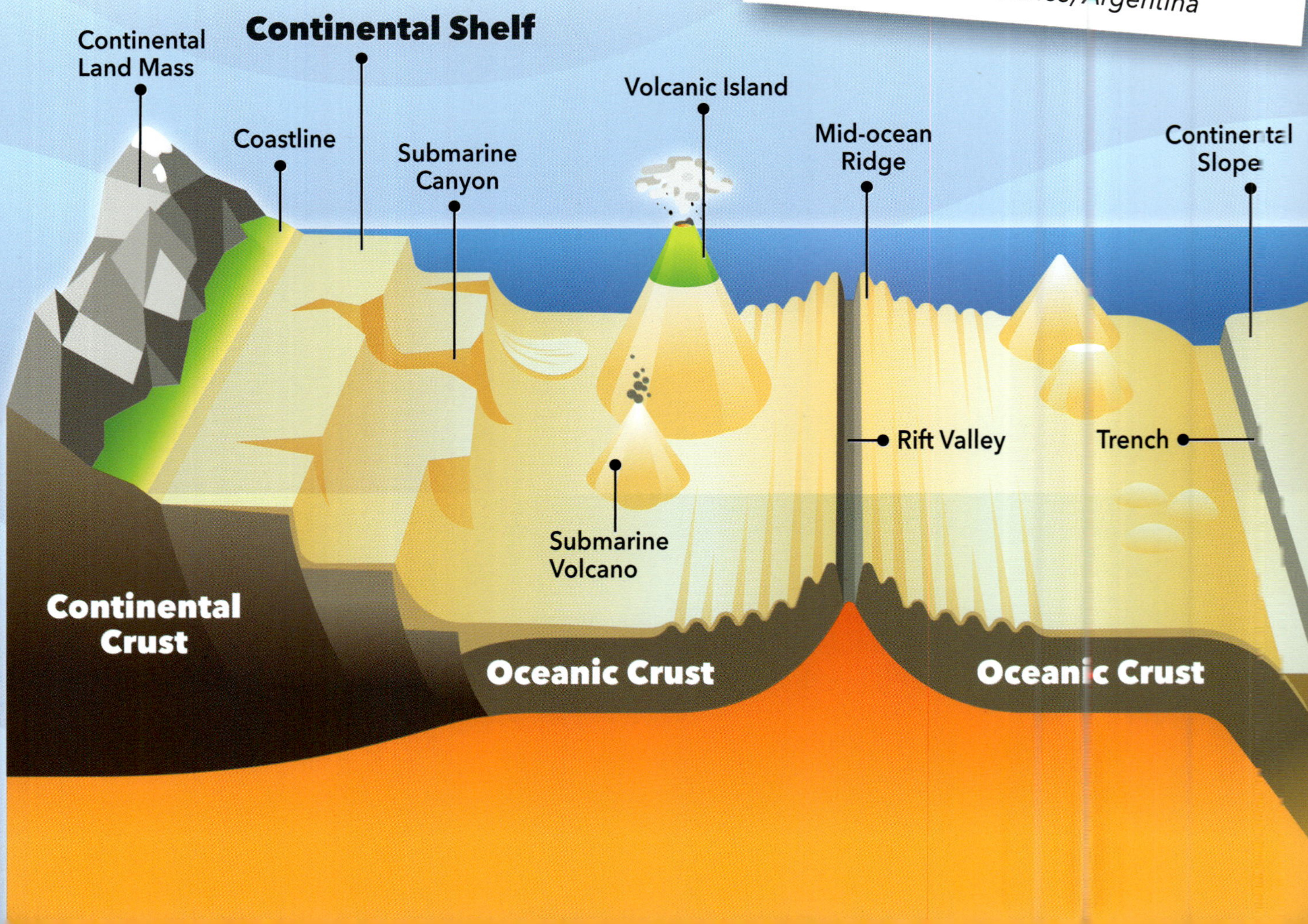

Where does a continent end?

At an ocean boundary, the UNCLOS Convention states that a nation has control over the ocean and the continental shelf for a distance of 200 nautical miles from the shore.

UNCLOS

The United Nations Convention on the Law of the Sea (UNCLOS) sets rules that countries use to determine who has control over the water and the seafloor at a nation's ocean boundary.

There are some coastlines that do not extend out into the ocean as underwater continental shelves

Where the rock is moving underneath other rocks at the edge of a continent, there is little or no continental shelf. This occurs along parts of South America's west coast. These sorts of places experience high levels of seismic activity, such as earthquakes and volcanic eruptions. As the two tectonic plates push against each other, they are lifting of the Andes mountain range.

In contrast, there is a large continental shelf off the east coast of Argentina. This enormous shelf has little tectonic activity and is considered to be very stable. It is the location of the Falkland Islands (also called the Malvinas Islands).

Landscapes

Alpine Areas

Although the Andes Mountains cross the Equator, there are cold, alpine conditions at their summit. Glaciers descend from the mountaintops, where the temperature is below freezing. Tropical rainforest and farms growing tropical produce take over from the alpine areas at lower altitudes.

Patagonian Desert

The Patagonian Desert is in the south of the continent, east of the Andes. It is a cold and dry desert, and is located in Argentina and Chile.

Rainforests

Tropical rainforests cover most of the northwest of South America, with the densest being in the area around the Amazon River. There are also smaller rainforests along parts of the eastern coast.

Brazilian Highlands

The Brazilian Highlands in the north of South America are rich in mineral resources.

Pampas

The Pampas are the broad, flat grasslands of Argentina. They are now extensively farmed for crop-growing and herding of livestock.

The Continent of South America

South America extends from Colombia in the north, down to Chile in the south. The most southerly point is Cape Horn.

Oceans around South America

South America is almost completely surrounded by water.

1. **Panama Isthmus** – Narrow piece of land where South America joins North America
2. **Caribbean Sea** – Northern border
3. **Atlantic Ocean** – Eastern border
4. **Pacific Ocean** – Western border
5. **Southern Ocean and Drake Passage** – Southernmost tip of South America

Countries with the largest and smallest populations in South America

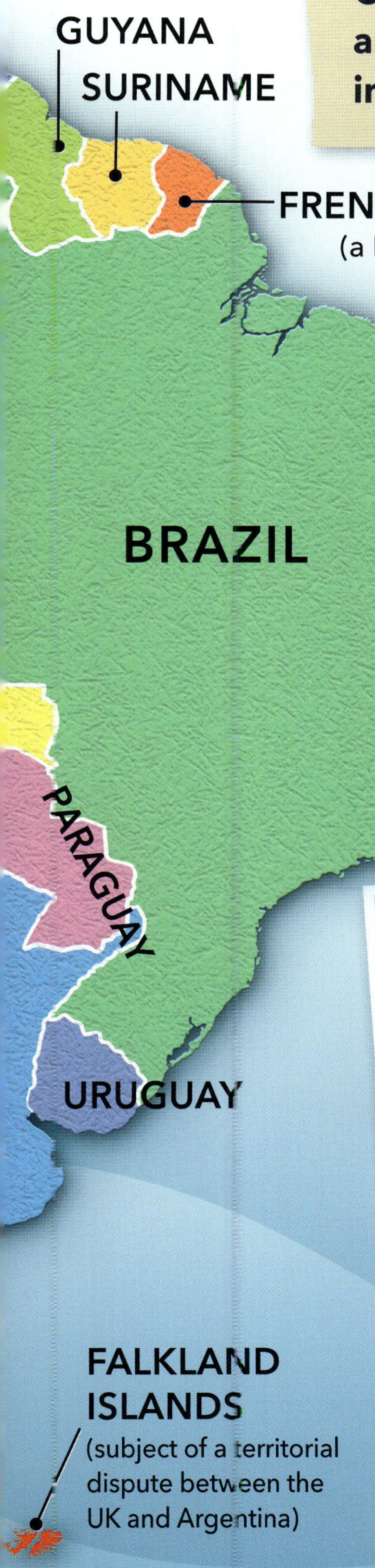

Brazil: over 212 million people

Colombia: over 51 million people

Falkland Islands: over 3,500 people

Agentina: over 45 million people

Highest Point

The highest point in South America is Mount Aconcagua, in Argentina, at nearly 7,000 metres high. It was a sacred mountain for the Inca people, and it is also the highest mountain outside Asia.

Volcanoes

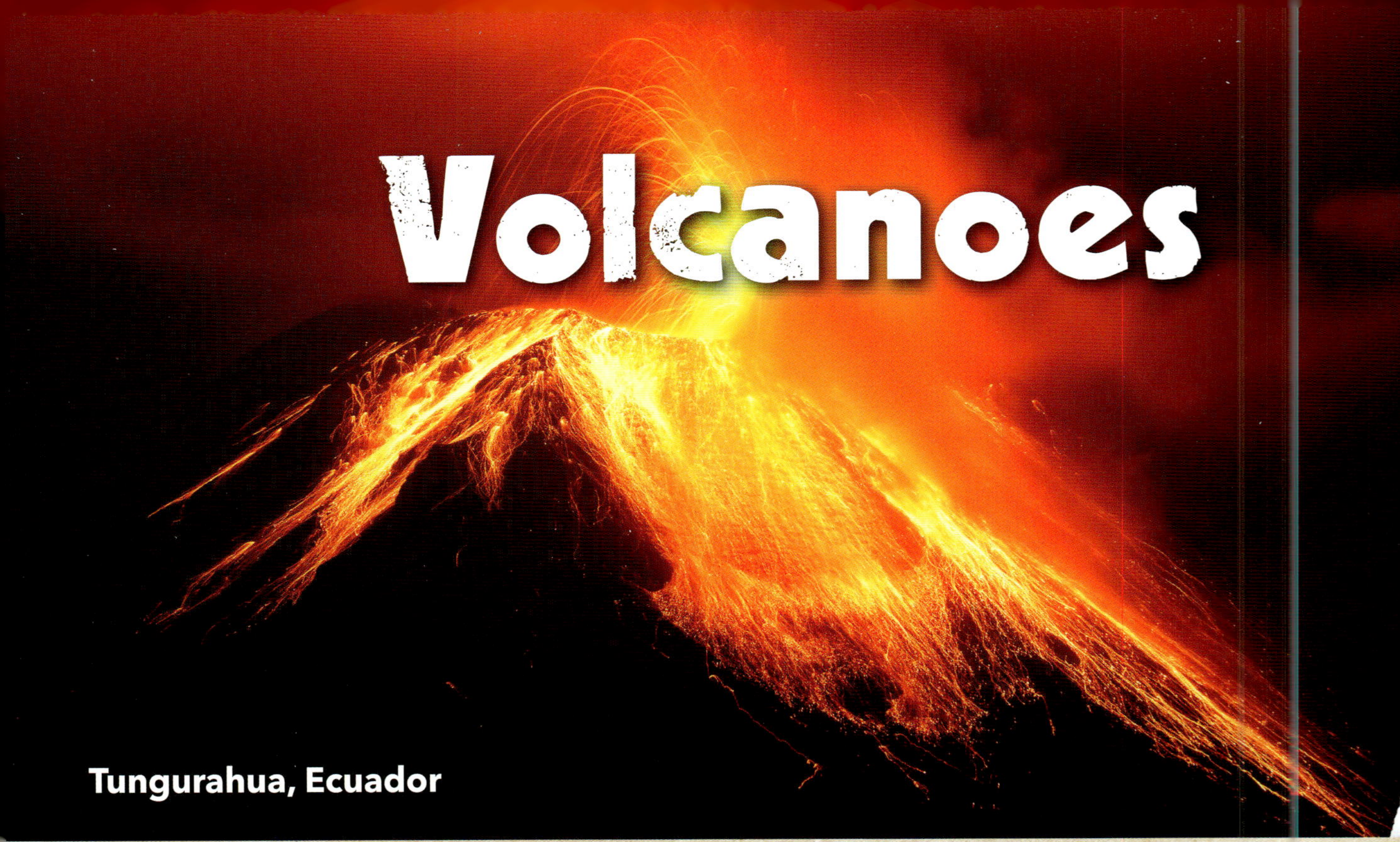

Tungurahua, Ecuador

South America is a volcanically active continent. Tectonic plate movement, causes the continued rise of the Andes Mountains and creates volcanoes along the length of the mountain range.

Cotopaxi, Ecuador

Reventador, Ecuador

Ojos del Salado, Argentina and Chile

The highest volcano in the world.

Nevado del Ruíz, Colombia

The volcano's summit is covered by glaciers that appear as a white mass surrounding the crater.

The Amazon

Amazon Rainforest

The Amazon rainforest has a legendary status and is one of the world's most treasured locations. This dense rainforest still covers most of the northwestern part of South America, although the demands of human population growth have resulted in large parts of the rainforest being cleared for farming, towns and homes for people.

Biodiverstity

The Amazon region has a unique biodiversity. It is home to millions of species of plants, animals and insects, and it is so dense that scientists think there may be many species that they have not yet discovered.

Amazon River

The Amazon River is one of the longest in the world. It rises in the Andes Mountains on the west of the continent, and flows all the way across to the east coast, gathering up the flow from many tributaries along the way. It empties its enormous load of fresh water into the Atlantic Ocean on the east coast of Brazil.

Coca is used to make anaesthetic

Over 25% of the world's medicines come from the Amazon rainforest.

Bark from the cinchona tree is used to treat malaria

The neuromuscular blocker tubocurarine is derived from moonseed plants

Indigenous Culture

At the time the first Spanish people arrived in the 1500s, the Amazon region was already inhabited by millions of indigenous people, who had a diverse range of cultures.

People of South America

Incas

The civilisations of the Incas flourished in South America before the arrival of the Spanish in the 1500s.

The Incas are sometimes represented today as being cruel, because of ancient religious practices which involved human sacrifice. However, they developed a distinctive art style and culture, and their buildings and stonework are amongst the most noteworthy examples of ancient architecture found anywhere in the world.

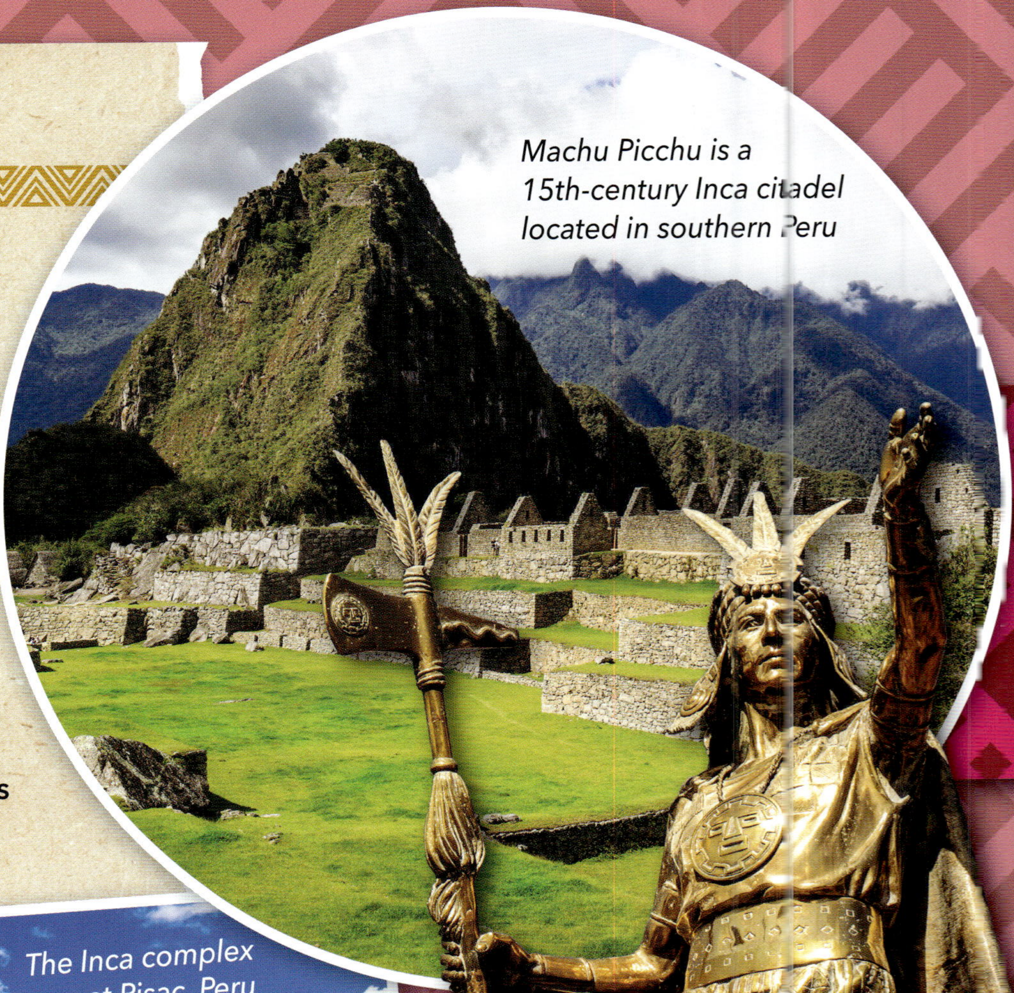

Machu Picchu is a 15th-century Inca citadel located in southern Peru

The Inca complex at Pisac, Peru

Statue of Pachacuti, an Incan Emperor in the 1400s

Ancestry

The Incan Empire ceased to exist after the arrival of the Spanish in the 1500s, but the Incan people survived. Many South Americans can trace their ancestors back to the ancient Incas.

South Americans Today

With their Spanish, Portuguese, African and South American indigenous heritage, the people of this continent manage to combine their cultural heritages to produce populations that are vibrant and unique.

Languages

Spanish and Portuguese are the most widely spoken languages in South America, but English is also used. German migrants settled in South America before and after the Second World War, resulting in German being a common language in some areas.

As well as European languages, there are also hundreds of indigenous languages still spoken across the continent.

Religion and Festivals

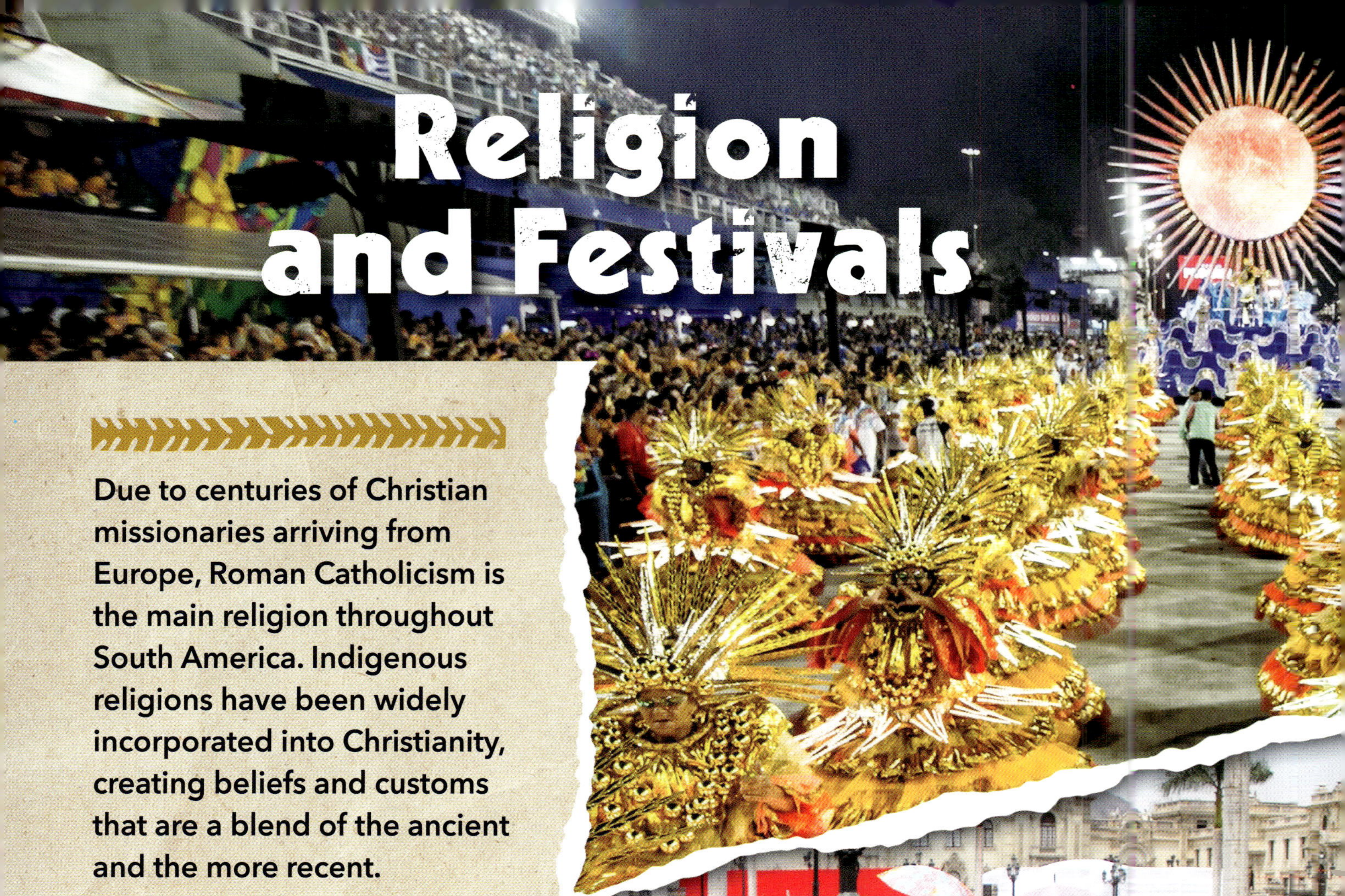

Due to centuries of Christian missionaries arriving from Europe, Roman Catholicism is the main religion throughout South America. Indigenous religions have been widely incorporated into Christianity, creating beliefs and customs that are a blend of the ancient and the more recent.

Festival of the Virgin of Candelaria

The second largest festival in South America, the Festival of The Virgin of Candelaria, is celebrated in Peru and Bolivia with music, dancing and magnificent costumes. The outstanding processions draw people from other areas, and normally quiet towns become crowded with visitors.

Rio Carnival

The Rio Carnival is held each year in Brazil. With a history that is related to the Christian period of Lent, this South American festival has developed into an event of processions, music, dancing and food. It is the largest carnival event held anywhere in the world.

Day of the Dead

Despite its name, this festival is a happy, lively occasion, during which people enjoy themselves while remembering their ancestors. A symbol of this festival is the decorated skull, which comes from a cultural tradition that dates from long before the arrival of the Spanish and Christianity. Although mainly a Mexican festival, many parts of South America also celebrate their own Day of the Dead.

Wildlife Wonders

Llamas and Alpacas

The llamas and alpacas of South America have evolved to live in high, cold altitudes. They were domesticated by the Incas, who used them for their wool and as pack animals. Like their camel relatives, these animals can survive with little water...and they spit when they are annoyed!

Capybara

Growing to over a metre in length, the capybara is the largest rodent in the world. It lives in the South American forests and likes to be near water.

Condor

The condor is a large bird of prey that lives in the high altitudes of the Andes Mountains. Their feathers are black and white, and they have a wingspan of over three metres. Condors can soar for hours, and they fly long distances in search of food.

Guinea Pigs

Guinea pigs were first domesticated from a wild ancestor in South America, where they are still bred as a source of food, not as pets.

Anaconda

The green anaconda can grow to an enormous size, reaching over five metres in length. It is a very strong snake that kills its prey by squeezing it.

Piranha

The piranha is a meat-eating fish that will attack animals it finds in the water. Represented in movies as a vicious hunter, the piranha certainly does have extremely sharp and strong teeth. Piranhas are quite small, growing to only about thirty centimetres, but they feed in large groups.

Nature's Bounty

From coffee to quinoa, South America abounds with natural produce.

Chocolate

Chocolate is made from cacao beans, which grow on cacao trees in the South American rainforest. The first people to collect and then grow cacao were the ancient Aztecs, Mayans and Incas. They used the beans to make a bitter drink. When Europeans took the beans back home, they added milk and sugar to make chocolate.

Eucalyptus Trees from Australia

Australian eucalyptus trees have been introduced into Peru in the past, and are now used as plantation trees for the supply of timber.

There are so many foods we love that originated in South America
Pineapples
Potatoes
Peanuts
Coffee
Passionfruit
Brazil Nuts
Cashew Nuts
Quinoa
Tomatoes

Economy of South America

Top Exporters

Brazil, Chile and Argentina are the top exporting nations in South America.

Frozen meat from Brazil

EXPORTS

Soybeans from Argentina

Copper ore from Chile

Mining

Copper from Chile and Peru is exported worldwide.

Coffee

Brazil is one of the world's largest producers of coffee beans.

Cattle Farming

South American cattle ranches are some of the largest anywhere in the world. The beef industry of Brazil is an important contributor to the South American economy.

Agriculture

Large parts of the natural forests and grasslands of South America are now cleared to provide land for agriculture and livestock farming.

Special Places in South America

1 Andes Mountains

The Andes Mountains run along the western coastal region of South America. Raised by the pushing together of two massive tectonic plates, the Andes include many volcanoes as well as geothermal areas of hot springs and geysers.

2 Strait of Magellan

The Strait of Magellan is a natural waterway between the lower east and west coasts of South America. It connects the Pacific and Atlantic Oceans. Using this route, ships can avoid having to sail around Cape Horn at the southern tip of the South American continent.

3 Lake Titicaca

Lake Titicaca is one of the largest lakes in South America. It is located high in the Andes, on the border between Bolivia and Peru. The Uru people of Lake Titicaca still keep their traditional lifestyle, and build their homes on floating reed mats.

4 Iguazu Falls

The vast Iguazu waterfalls are now a World Heritage Site. They separate the upper and lower sections of the Iguazu River and are over three kilometres in width, spanning the border between Argentina and Brazil. The water cascades into a narrow canyon from a long horseshoe shape at the edge of an 80 metre high plateau.

5 Machu Picchu

This small settlement on the top of a hill in a remote part of Peru was abandoned by its Incan inhabitants in the 1500s. The stonework and engineering are remarkable, especially considering that the people who built Machu Picchu only had stone tools to work with.

6 Rainbow Mountain, Peru

The striking colours of Rainbow Mountain or Vinicunca in Peru are a result of millions of years of mountain building activity in the region. Sediments were laid down and then lifted to create the stripes, and weathering helped to produce all the different colours. The colours of Vinicunca only became apparent a few years ago, as snow that used to cover them began to melt.

7 Galapagos Islands

Located west of Ecuador, the Galapagos Islands are one of the world's most important places of biodiversity. The isolation of the wildlife provided Charles Darwin with an opportunity to study the process of evolution, which led to him writing his momentous book, *On the Origin Of Species*.

8 Easter Island (Rapa Nui), Chile

Although Easter Island is not physically part of the South American continent, the island is now a part of Chile. It lies thousands of kilometres west of Chile in the Pacific Ocean. Easter Island is famous for its large stone statues, called Moai, erected by the Rapa Nui people about a thousand years ago. It is still a mystery how they managed to move such large stones.

9 Bogota, Colombia

12 Rio de Janeiro, Brazil

10 Lima, Peru

Capital Cities

The size of a large city can be measured either by its area, the population of its city centre, or the population including its suburbs.

Taking all of these into account, these are the largest cities in South America:

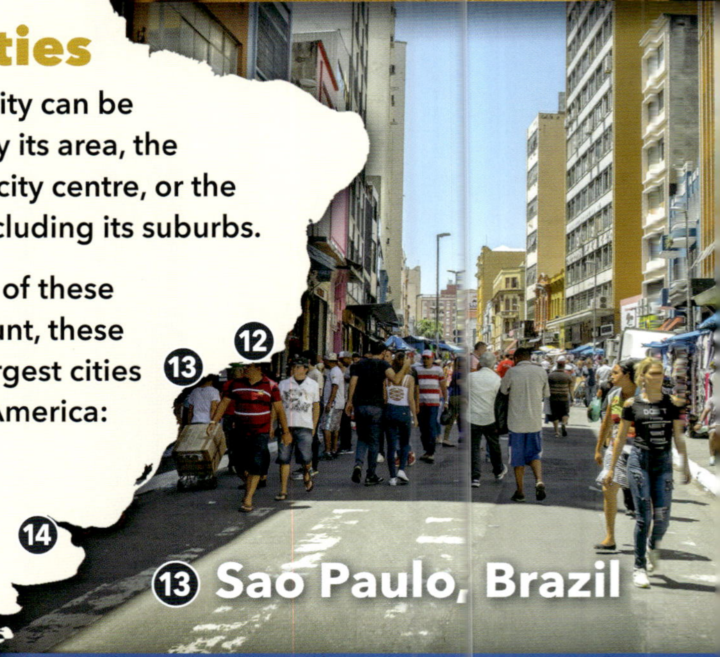

13 Sao Paulo, Brazil

11 Santiago, Chile

14 Buenos Aires, Argentina

Glossary

Alpine climates have very cold temperatures

alpine climate very cold or freezing temperatures, with snow and ice, and cool summers

altitude height above sea level

biodiversity range of plants and animals in an area

citadel fortified town where people can seek shelter

continental shelf edges of a continent that extend outwards under the water

Equator imaginary line around the middle of the Earth

geothermal area area affected by heat rising from beneath the surface of the Earth

geyser a spring that periodically erupts with hot water

isthmus narrow piece of land, with water on both sides, connecting two larger landmasses

nautical mile measurement of distance over water or when travelling in the air. It equals 1.85 kilometres

ocean abyss very deep part of an ocean

plate tectonics movement of large blocks of land across the Earth

seismic relating to earthquakes

tropical climate very hot, humid climate, with high rainfall, found at and near the Equator

vibrant lively

The Amazon region has a unique biodiversity

Rio Carnival

Index

Easter Island